Michelle Brown

Notes and activities by Gina D. B. Clemen

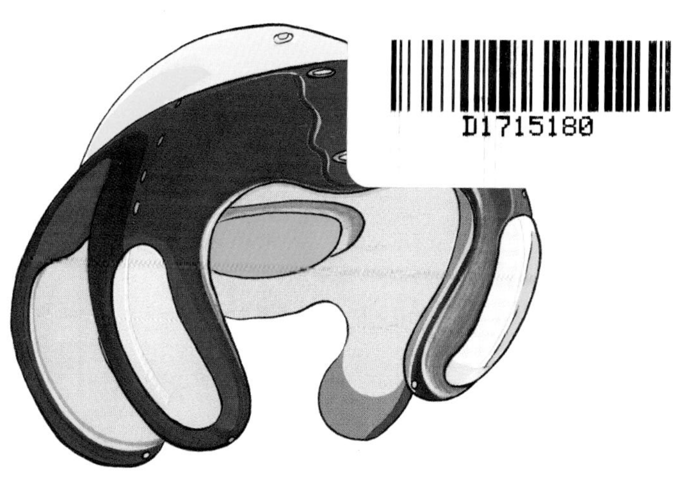

Editors: Rebecca Raynes, Elvira Poggi Repetto
Design: Nadia Maestri
Illustrations: Mario Benvenuto

First edition: May 1998

We would be happy to receive your comments and suggestions, and give you any other information concerning our material.
editorial@blackcat-cideb.com
www.blackcat-cideb.com
www.cideb.it

ISBN 88-7754-757-X

Printed in Italy by Litoprint, Genoa

Contents

This story is recorded in full on the cassette.

These symbols indicate the beginning and end of the extracts linked to the listening activities.

CHAPTER 1

The New Teacher

My name is Jennifer Dale. My friends call me Jenny. I'm 16 years old and I live near Boston. My town is beautiful and very green. I live here with my parents and my dog, Fred. I go to school at Jefferson High and I want to become a journalist. In my free time I play volleyball and I listen to "heavy metal" music.

I want to tell you my story.

It was the first day of high school. I was excited. I already knew most of my classmates, but I didn't know my new teachers. I got up, ate my breakfast and went to school. On the street I met my friend, Dana; her house is near mine and we always walk to school together.

"I hope our new teachers are men. And I hope they're handsome!" Dana said. Dana loves talking about boys.

Alien at School

"Yes, I need something new and interesting in my life," I answered.

We arrived at school and went into our classroom. A young man was inside.

"Hello, boys and girls. I'm your new science teacher. My name is Mr Adams. I hope to work well with you this year."

Dana and I looked at Mr Adams. He was tall and thin. He had blond hair and brown eyes. He seemed friendly.

"We're lucky! I think he's a very handsome teacher!" Dana said to me.

"Yes, he is!" I answered. I looked at him and he looked at me. Our eyes met.

"What's your name?" he asked, smiling.

"Uh, Jennifer," I answered. I was a little nervous.

He turned to Dana. "And who are you?"

"I'm Dana!" Dana gave him a big, enthusiastic smile. At that moment the noise of an airplane [1] attracted our attention. Everyone in the class looked out of the window, but the sun was in front of us. It bothered [2] our eyes. We turned away from the window. Except Mr Adams. He was at the window and was looking directly at the sun. The sun didn't irritate his eyes!

1. **airplane** : B.E. aeroplane.
2. **bothered** : disturbed.

The New Teacher

"Gee!" [1] I thought, "How can he look at it like that?!!"

The airplane then passed and the lesson continued. When the hour finished, another man walked in. This one had black hair and green eyes. His nose was small and pointed, and he had strangely high cheekbones. [2]

"What a weird [3]-looking teacher!" I said to Dana.

1. **Gee!** : American expression of surprise.
2. **cheekbones** :
3. **weird** [wɪəd] : strange, bizarre.

Alien at School

"Wow, you're right!" she exclaimed.

The teacher didn't smile and spoke coldly to the class.

"I'm your English teacher. I want you to be on your best behaviour this year. The lesson can begin. And remember, no talking!"

Everyone in class was evidently shocked, but no one said anything. Another student, Steve, raised his hand.

"What?" asked the new teacher in his cold voice.

"Excuse me, but what's your name?"

"Mr Stone," he answered. I then noticed that his voice wasn't just cold: it was metallic and monotonous! Dana looked at me with disappointment. She raised her eyebrows. "What's his problem?" she mouthed. [1]

The lesson proceeded. Mr Stone read a poem from our English Literature book. His voice was weird, very weird. It had no emotion. It was almost robotic!

Someone touched me. It was Dana. "Isn't he horrible?" she whispered. I nodded.

The other teachers we met that morning were Miss Smith, the arts teacher, and Mrs Ching, who taught math. [2] Both seemed nice. Miss Smith, in particular, was a very cheerful [3] person.

1. **mouthed** : pronounced words using the lips but not the voice.
2. **math** : B.E. maths.
3. **cheerful** : happy.

1 **Give an identikit of the main character.**

Name: ....

Age: ....

School: ....

Aspirations: ....

Hobbies: ....

Now give an identikit of yourself.

Name: ....

Age: ....

School: ....

Aspirations: ....

Hobbies: ....

2 **Answer the following questions.**

a. Who is Dana?

b. Who is Mr Adams?

c. What distracts the attention of the class?

d. As a teacher how is Mr Stone different from Mr Adams?

e. Write five adjectives that describe Mr Stone's voice.

3 **List the physical traits of Mr Adams and Mr Stone.**

MR ADAMS	MR STONE
....	....
....	....
....	....
....	....

4 **Nouns are often used to create adjectives and adverbs.**

NOUN	ADJECTIVE	ADVERB
science →	scientific →	scientifically

Can you fill in the chart with the missing words?

NOUN	ADJECTIVE	ADVERB
poverty		
	lucky	
		happily
honesty		
	courageous	
elegance		
		angrily
	musical	

5 **How was your first day of school this year?**

☐ fun ☐ frightening ☐ boring ☐ unhappy ☐ interesting

Why? ....

6 What do you do during the school day? Fill in this timetable.

6:30 am I get up and I...	
7:00	5:00
8:00	
9:00	7:00
Noon	9:00
1:00	
	11:00
3:00	

For discussion and writing

7 Now write a paragraph about your day yesterday.

8 Describe your best friend or a school friend, and say what you like about him/her.

CHAPTER 2

Clues

I always eat lunch at school. That day I ate with Dana and Paul Miller, another friend from my class. Paul was a very intelligent boy. He was always the best in math. His parents were divorced and he lived with his father and his black cat, Apollo. He missed his mother. She lived with another man and didn't want to see Paul. His father was never at home, so Paul was very lonely. He didn't have many friends at school because he was too intellectual. He loved Apollo very much and spent a lot of time with him.

Clues

"What do you think about our new teachers?" I asked my friends.

"I think Mr Adams is very sexy!" said Dana.

"Did you see how he looked at the airplane? The sun didn't bother him!" exclaimed Paul. "You're right!" I said. "But did you hear Mr Stone? He speaks like a robot! His voice is cold and metallic!"

"He's unfriendly too!" added Dana.

"That's true!" I said.

"Look!" said Paul. "Look what he's eating!" We looked at Mr Stone. He sat away from the other teachers and he didn't have a normal lunch. There was a glass in front of him. It was full of a dense, green liquid. There were some black pills in his hand. He put two of them in the glass. The green liquid started to bubble, and it changed colour: it started to become red! Then he took the glass and drank the mysterious red formula.

I looked at Paul and he looked at me. We were disgusted and frightened. Dana tried to be rational. “Maybe it’s a new diet. Maybe that’s why he’s so thin!” she said. I didn’t agree. There was something strange about Mr Stone.

That afternoon and the next day we met our other new teachers. We also had English again. Mr Stone came in and sat down.

“Miller. Paul Miller. Tell me something about yourself.”

Paul was surprised. English teachers don’t usually ask personal questions!

“Well, Paul? Don’t you have anything to say?”

“Uh, well, I enjoy astronomy, I have a cat...” Mr Stone asked everyone to say something about their life and hobbies.

“Maybe he wants to create a relationship with us, but he’s such a cold person! How bizarre!” I thought. Then, looking at him more carefully, I noticed something: his eyes weren’t green anymore! They seemed a darker, different colour! I raised my hand.

“May I go to the bathroom?” I asked. As I walked towards the door, I looked at Mr Stone’s eyes again. I was right! They were yellowish brown. They looked like amber!

benvenuto

What happened in Chapter Two?

1 **a.** Why was Paul very lonely?
b. Describe Mr Stone's lunch.
c. How did Mr Stone begin his second English lesson?
d. Why did Jenny want to go to the bathroom?

2 **Are these sentences true (T) or false (F)? Correct the false ones.**

		T	F
a.	Paul's best subject at school was English.	☐	☐
b.	Mr Stone's strange drink became red.	☐	☐
c.	Mr Stone wasn't interested in the students' personal life.	☐	☐
d.	Mr Stone's eye colour changed from amber to green.	☐	☐

Countable or uncountable?

3 **Put these words in the correct table.**

time pills eyes meat water friends milk fruit clothes food hobbies people

MUCH	MANY

4 **There are 14 verbs from Chapters 1 and 2 in this word puzzle. Can you find and circle them? Then write their Past Simple form and Past Participle in the correct column.**

G	S	I	L	E	P	M	O	F	C	S	A	Q
M	E	A	T	Y	Z	A	D	S	X	P	G	B
I	R	T	O	F	Q	P	R	I	C	E	U	D
P	B	H	N	T	E	L	L	G	W	A	V	S
V	E	E	R	G	T	E	K	R	V	K	B	I
E	G	J	C	J	M	Q	H	O	H	Q	Y	T
A	I	R	T	O	B	E	K	N	O	W	D	V
E	N	F	A	H	M	I	E	V	D	F	G	Q
Z	G	O	K	H	A	E	J	T	H	I	N	K
H	D	L	E	A	H	A	V	E	B	R	U	S

INFINITIVE	PAST SIMPLE	PAST PARTICIPLE

For discussion and writing

5 **Why do you think Mr Stone has such a strange lunch?**

6 **Do you think Mr Stone's eyes changed colour or was it Jenny's imagination?**

Before you read

1 Listen to the first part of Chapter 3. Then listen to it again and fill in the gaps.

That afternoon I sat on my .... and thought about my first .... days of high school. I wanted to know more about Mr .... I decided to go and visit Paul.

Paul was in front of his .... He was very interested in astronomy, the ...., and life on other planets.

"Hi, Paul. What are you doing?" I asked.

"I'm on the .... I'm in contact with the International Space Fan .... Listen to this. Something very important is happening. A .... is passing through the Virgo constellation. There are the right connections for intergalactic ....! The Earth has been in the Virgo constellation since last ...."

"But what are intergalactic meetings?" I asked.

"They're .... of aliens to our planet. These voyages can happen only in special .... , for example, when a constellation and a comet meet. .... can travel to our planet for different reasons. Sometimes they want to study us .... Some people say that aliens may come to Earth to conquer the ...."

CHAPTER 3

Aliens

That afternoon I sat on my bed and thought about my first two days of high school. I wanted to know more about Mr Stone. I decided to go and visit Paul.

Paul was in front of his computer. He was very interested in astronomy, the occult, and life on other planets.

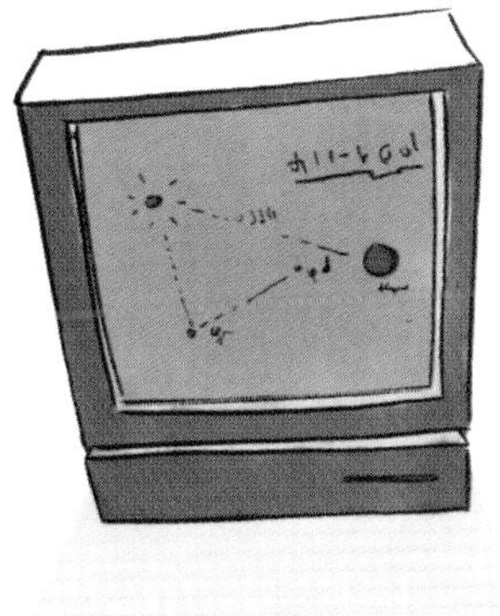

"Hi, Paul. What are you doing?" I asked.

"I'm on the Internet. I'm in contact with the International Space Fan Club. Listen to this. Something very important is happening. A comet is passing

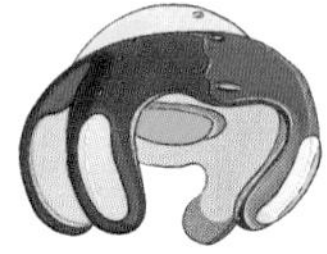

through the Virgo constellation. There are the right connections for intergalactic meetings! The Earth has been in the Virgo constellation since last week."

"But what are intergalactic meetings?" I asked.

"They're voyages of aliens to our planet. These voyages can happen only in special moments, for example, when a constellation and a comet meet. Aliens can travel to our planet for different reasons. Sometimes they want to study us humans. Some people say that aliens may come to Earth to conquer the planet."

I looked at Paul with a shocked expression. An idea started to form in my mind.

"What's wrong, Jenny?" Paul asked.

"Maybe Mr Stone is an alien!" I exclaimed.

"Gee, aren't you exaggerating? Come on, get real!!" [1]

"Well, his voice doesn't seem human, his eyes change colour, and do you remember the green liquid and the black pills he had for lunch?"

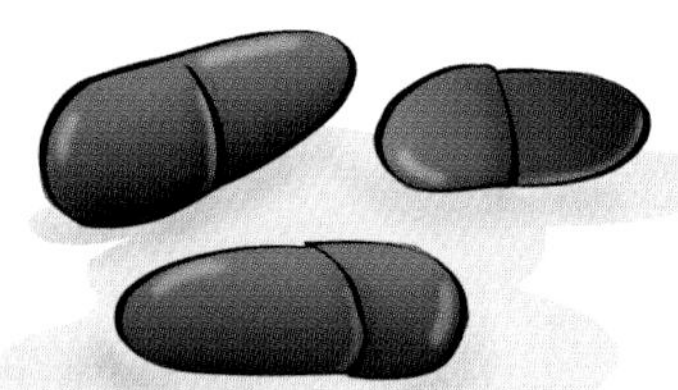

"What do you mean, his eyes change colour?" Paul asked.

"Didn't you notice? Yesterday they were green; today they're amber-coloured!" I answered.

1. **get real!** : American expression for "be reasonable" or "be realistic".

Aliens

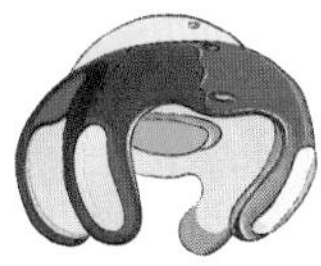

"Even if his eyes change colour, I still don't believe he's an alien."

"But the comet explains everything: it entered the Virgo constellation last week, and Mr Stone *is* a new teacher. I talked to Dana's brother, Matt. He said that this is Mr Stone's first year at Jefferson High. No one knows where he comes from!" I said.

"Maybe..." Paul's eyes lit up. [1] "Maybe that's why he asked us all those personal questions: he wants to study us!"

"Yes! You see, all clues indicate that he *is* an alien! So, what can we do?" I asked.

"We can spy on him. Maybe we can follow him to his house. We can see where he lives and what he does at home. However, we must be very careful. He doesn't seem to have emotions. He might get angry if he discovers we suspect him. We'll try to follow him tomorrow, after school, OK?" said Paul.

The next morning before school, I took Fred out for a walk in the park. Fred needs daily exercise, so my parents and I take turns [2] walking the dog.

The park was empty. It was dawn. A lonely bird chirped [3]

1. **lit up** : (past simple of "light up") became bright.
2. **take turns** : alternate.
3. **chirped** [tʃɜːrpt] : (for birds) sang.

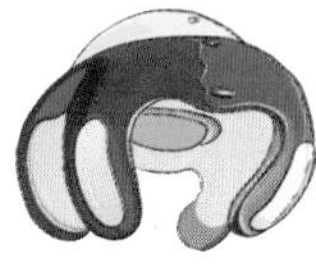

in the trees. The grass was wet with dew. [1] There was peace all around.

Suddenly, I noticed something, or someone, moving behind the bushes. I got closer to see who, or what, it was.

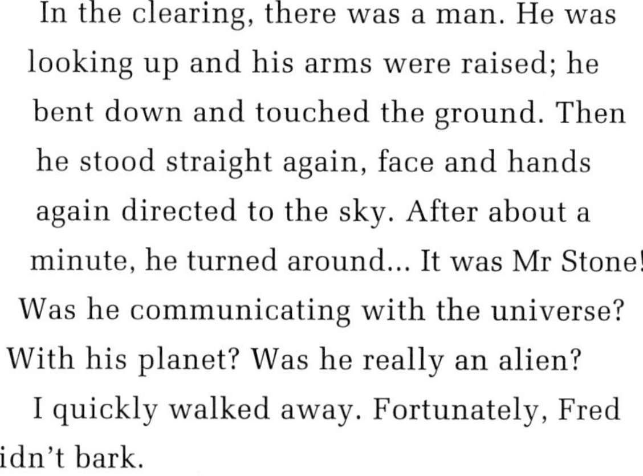

In the clearing, there was a man. He was looking up and his arms were raised; he bent down and touched the ground. Then he stood straight again, face and hands again directed to the sky. After about a minute, he turned around... It was Mr Stone! Was he communicating with the universe? With his planet? Was he really an alien?

I quickly walked away. Fortunately, Fred didn't bark.

I took my dog home and then met Dana. We walked to school. I wanted to tell her about Mr Stone, but I didn't. It was too difficult. Besides, I couldn't tell her about the afternoon plan, because it was too dangerous for three people to follow the teacher.

During the morning I thought about Mr Stone again and again. I was scared, [2] but also excited.

1. **dew** : small drops of water.
2. **scared** : frightened, nervous.

What happened in Chapter Three?

1 **a.** What are intergalactic meetings?
b. What was Jenny's shocking idea?
c. What did Jenny and Paul decide to do?
d. What was Mr Stone doing in the park?

2 **Complete the following table.**

	ADJECTIVE	COMPARATIVE	SUPERLATIVE
IRREGULAR	good		the best
	bad	worse	
REGULAR	warm		
		faster	
			the smartest
	light		
			the nicest
		heavier	
	noisy		
		happier	
			the highest

Word puzzle

3 Find a word for each clue.

a. The earth is a ....
b. The centre of the solar system is the ....
c. The strange creature from outer space is an ....
d. The group of stars that form a picture in the sky is a ....
e. The space between trees is a ....
f. A bright celestial body with a head and tail is a ....
g. The science that studies the sun, moon, stars and planets is ....

For discussion and writing

4 **a.** What's your opinion of the Internet?
b. List its positive and negative aspects.
c. Do you believe in alien life? Why or why not?
d. How do you imagine an alien?

- ☐ technologically advanced
- ☐ physically bizarre
- ☐ evil and powerful
- ☐ friendly and helpful
- ☐ other ....

UFOs

Unidentified Flying Objects, UFOs, have been sighted by people all over the world for a long time. About 40 sightings are reported every day! These mysterious flying objects have been filmed, photographed and discussed at length.

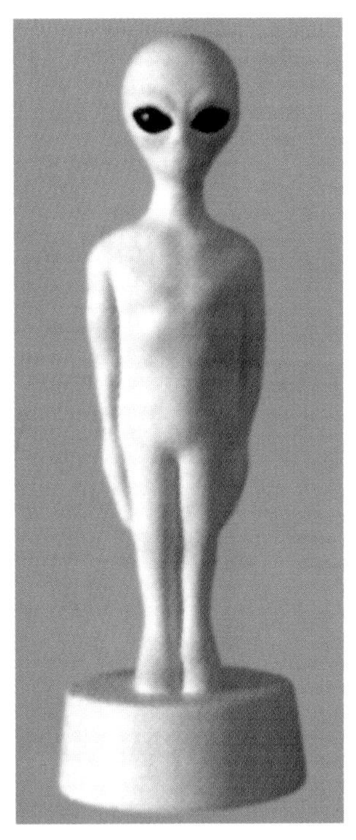

People have even reported visits with aliens on a UFO! Often the photos of UFOs were fakes [1] and the films were hoaxes. [2]

Every year many international conferences are held by ufologists to investigate and study the latest sightings and UFO news.

Do UFOs really exist or are they figments of people's imaginations? There can be many explanations for bright lights and strangely shaped objects that suddenly appear in the sky. They could be bright aeroplane lights, secret military aircraft, satellites, weather balloons, meteors, strange cloud

1. **fakes** : (here) something that is not what it seems to be.
2. **hoaxes** : tricks.

shapes, reflections or even hallucinations! Of course, they could also be UFOs!

Sightings are divided into four categories:

1. CE-1K – Close encounters of the first kind are UFO sightings in the sky or on the ground, with no permanent evidence. Almost all UFO sightings are of this kind and most can be explained scientifically.
2. CE-2K – Close encounters of the second kind are sightings with permanent evidence, such as burn marks on the ground or grass, a watch that stops or a car engine that turns off.
3. CE-3K – Close encounters of the third kind are sightings of aliens from a UFO, but usually without meeting them.
4. CE-4K – Close encounters of the fourth kind are real meetings with aliens, or a visit on board their UFO.

Reports of sightings started a long time ago. An old story says that Alexander the Great and his army saw "silver shields" flying in the sky in the year 329 BC.

Birthplace of the UFO era

EO journalist broke first 'flying saucer' story

Another legend tells us that the Roman writer Livy saw flying objects in the sky in 218 BC. He called these "flying altars".

It seems that the scholars and monks of the Middle Ages wrote

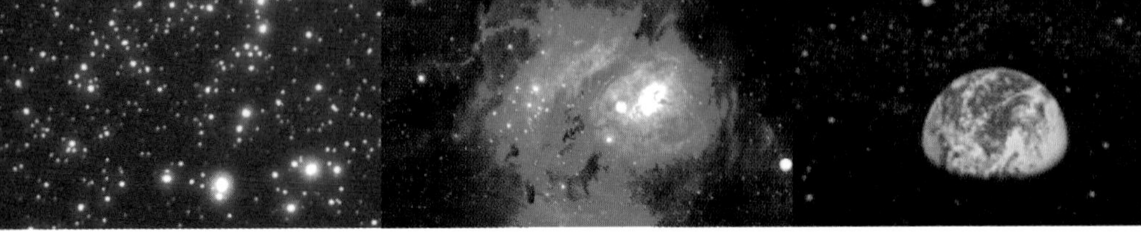

about "strange and mysterious objects" flying in the night sky!

One of the first important sightings in the United States was in Sacramento, California. One November day in 1896 about 200 people said they saw a big UFO flying over them. Newspapers all over the United States talked about this extraordinary event for weeks. During this period there were many sightings everywhere.

The term "flying saucer", [1] to indicate a strange flying object, was born on 24 June 1947. Kenneth Arnold, an American pilot, was flying over the Cascade Mountains in the western United States. Suddenly, he noticed nine silver discs flying at about 1900 kilometres an hour! When he returned to his air base he immediately told the newspapers about the "flying saucers" he had seen. From that moment, Arnold became famous all over the world. This was the beginning of the modern UFO era.

Several United States Air Force pilots and astronauts have reported seeing UFOs during their flights. In 1965 U.S. astronauts James

1. **saucer** [sɔːsə] : small plate on which you put a cup.

McDivitt and Ed White were orbiting around the earth in their spaceship. During their trip they reported seeing a UFO, and McDivitt filmed it and took several photos. No one has ever seen the photos or the film.

The phenomenon of UFOs and aliens is an exciting one to explore.

If you're interested and want to contact a UFO study group, here are two addresses and a web site:

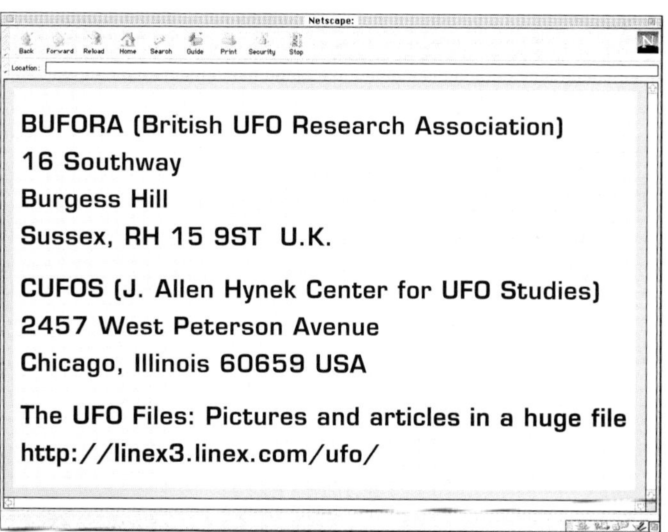

1 Choose the correct answer.

a. How many UFO sightings are reported everyday?
- ☐ 20
- ☐ 400
- ☐ 40

b. Ufologists are people who
- ☐ communicate with other planets
- ☐ study and investigate UFO sightings
- ☐ study the stars

c. A CE-2K is a sighting
- ☐ with permanent evidence
- ☐ in the sky or on the ground
- ☐ of a friendly alien

d. Today ufologists divide UFO sightings into
- ☐ 2 kinds
- ☐ 4 kinds
- ☐ 8 kinds

e. Kenneth Arnold was
- ☐ an American astronaut
- ☐ a British ufologist
- ☐ an American pilot

f. He was the first person to use the term
- ☐ flying saucer
- ☐ flying ship
- ☐ UFO

g. In 1965 two U.S. astronauts
- ☐ visited a UFO in space
- ☐ sighted three UFOs during their orbit around the earth
- ☐ sighted, photographed and filmed a UFO during their orbit around the earth

Word search

2 Discuss with a classmate what things you can find in the sky, and then try and find six of these things in the word puzzle.

R	B	S	F	G	I	D	P	B	C	R	G	V
C	Y	P	R	B	E	K	V	S	A	O	K	S
L	O	A	A	I	R	P	L	A	N	E	L	H
O	P	C	B	A	Q	C	G	T	I	V	C	X
U	Z	E	A	S	X	Y	J	E	M	A	J	F
D	V	C	Q	L	T	J	S	L	O	S	R	P
V	B	R	U	N	Z	A	B	L	I	X	U	W
H	G	A	W	I	G	H	R	I	N	J	T	N
E	M	F	D	O	B	D	P	T	D	B	G	F
X	B	T	G	E	H	K	S	E	V	C	H	Y

CHAPTER 4

Too Much Imagination?

When the science class started, Mr Adams walked in.

"Come on, boys and girls. Today we're going to the science laboratory!" he announced.

In our lab there are some white mice and some hamsters [1] in cages. As Mr Adams passed by their cages, they started to squeal [2] loudly. They were very agitated. Mr Adams laughed. "What's wrong?" he said, speaking to the animals. "I won't eat you!"

1. **hamsters** : small animals that resemble mice but have no tails.
2. **squeal** : make a long, sharp cry.

Too Much Imagination?

Then he gave us some worms. "You must cut them into little pieces. The pieces can live and move independently," he said.

I looked at my worm. It was pale and slimy.[1] I didn't want to cut it up.

"Jennifer. Are you afraid of cutting up your worm?" I looked up. Mr Adams was at my desk. He smiled down at me. "Give me your knife." I thanked him and gave it to him. His arm touched mine. It tickled.[2] An electric shock ran through me and I jumped.

"What's wrong?" asked Mr Adams. He seemed frightened.

"N-Nothing," I answered, trying to smile. He helped me cut up my worm, then walked away. No one else in class had noticed anything. I didn't know what to think. Were all my teachers weird, or was I just too imaginative?

I wrote a note to Paul and told him what had happened.

1. **slimy** [slaɪmi] : covered with a thick, unpleasant liquid.
2. **tickled** : touched a part of the body and produced a strange sensation.

"Paul!" I whispered. Paul turned and looked at me. I passed the note.

"Excuse me. What are you doing? Paul, what do you have in your hand?" asked Mr Adams. His voice made me freeze. [1] We were in very big trouble.

"N-N-Nothing," said Paul.

"Please listen to the lesson. If I see you again, you must give me the note."

"I'm sorry," answered Paul.

WHEW!! [2] I was so happy that I wanted to laugh. Obviously, I didn't.

When the bell rang, Mr Adams called me to his desk. "Oh, no... ," I thought.

He smiled. "I'm sorry I scared you; two years ago I had an accident. My left arm is artificial. It's an electric prosthesis and sometimes it can give electric shocks." He seemed a little embarrassed.

I was surprised and sorry; he was so sweet! I thanked him and went to lunch.

"Paul, forget what I wrote," I said, as I sat down at our usual lunch table. I told Paul and Dana about Mr Adams' electric prosthesis. Then Dana mentioned Mr Stone. Paul and I

1. **freeze** : (here) stop suddenly, become very still.
2. **whew** [fhju:] : expression of relief or surprise.

looked at each other, but we didn't say anything. Besides, after school, Dana had a dance club meeting in the gym, so Paul and I were free.

We finished our chocolate milk and went out to recess. [1] At the door we met Mr Stone. His head was down; he seemed deep in thought.

"Hi!" Dana said to him.

"Oh. Uh, hi... ," he said, surprised, lifting his head. His eyes were green again!

"Wow, that Mr Stone is really a mystery!" Dana exclaimed.

I still didn't want to tell Dana the whole story, so I changed the subject. Fortunately, the bell interrupted us. Before entering class at one o'clock, I took Paul aside. I quickly told him about what I had seen in the park.

"Wow... I wonder what we'll see this afternoon!" remarked Paul.

1. **recess** : American expression for the break between lessons.

What happened in Chapter Four?

1 **a.** Why did the laboratory animals squeal?
b. Why did Mr Adams give worms to the class?
c. What was Mr Adams's problem?
d. What did Jenny notice about Mr Stone when she saw him in the cafeteria?

2 **Unscramble the words in italics and then put the sentences in chronological order.**

a. ☐ Jenny didn't want to cut up her *mrow* ....
b. ☐ Mr Adams gave Jenny an *terielcc* .... shock.
c. ☐ The lab animals *dleuasqe* .... when Mr Adams passed.
d. ☐ Mr Adams called Jenny to his *sked* ....
e. ☐ Jenny wrote a *tneo* .... to Paul.
f. ☐ Jenny gave her *fenik* .... to Mr Adams.

3 **Mr Stone and Mr Adams are both teachers. Write a brief description of all the jobs below.**

a. doctor ....
....
b. engineer ....
....
c. musician ....
....
d. pilot ....
....
e. sports champion ....
....

f. journalist ....

....

g. teacher ....

....

h. actor/actress ....

....

i. scientist ....

....

j. writer ....

....

k. manager ....

....

l. architect ....

....

4 **Circle the 3 jobs you prefer on the list.**

5 **What kind of job would you like to do and why?**

....

....

Prediction

6 **What do you think Paul and Jenny will see when they follow Mr Stone to his house?**

7 **Do you think he will notice them?**

American Teenagers and High School

Life in an American high school is an exciting and stimulating learning experience. High school in America is not just a scholastic centre. It is also an important social centre, where students can develop other interests and talents.

Let's see how!

Each American high school has its school colours, school motto and school ring. Students can buy clothing and accessories with the school colours and motto.

The high school course is divided into four years, and each year has a specific name. In the first year you're called a freshman, in the second year, a sophomore, in the third year, a junior, and in the fourth year, a senior. The typical teenager starts school at about 8:00 a.m. (starting time can vary from school to school), and ends at about 3 p.m. There's no school on Saturday. Every student has a locker, which is a small metal closet where

coats, books, sports equipment and other personal things are kept. Each locker has a combination lock.

Students have lunch at the school cafeteria, where they can choose from a variety of good things to eat and drink. After lunch students go outside to the school recreation area to play a sport, to talk to friends or simply to relax. The lunch break lasts about an hour.

When the school day ends some students go home, but many remain at school for after-school activities. There are many activities and clubs to choose from. Clubs meet on specific afternoons.

Here are some typical after-school clubs:

The Drama Club	which prepares school plays and other theatrical events;
The Journalism Club	which prepares the school newspaper and year book;
The Science Club	which does experiments in the Science Laboratory;
The Aerobics Club	which practices aerobics;
The Art Club	which creates paintings, drawings, sculptures for exhibits.

There is always a teacher present at club meetings. With the principal's [1] approval, students can start any kind of club that is educational and fun!

In the afternoon many students practise sports with the school team. Sports are an important part of high school life. Schools have a modern gymnasium and a big outdoor sports area. Every high school has either a football, basketball, baseball, volleyball or swimming team. Most have all these sports and many more! It's an honour to play on the school team.

Cheerleaders are girls who dress in special uniforms with the school colours and are present at all the sports activities. They coordinate the cheering!

1. **principal** : head of a school or college.

American high school students like to be "popular". This means being a good student, being active in the community and being well-liked by others. Popular students are elected to participate in student government. Every year in June there are prizes for the best students and the best athletes.

There are many social events during the school year which involve[1] the entire school and the teachers. Look at these events:

- Halloween Party and Dance on October 31
- Christmas Fund Raiser – students help the poor of the community at Christmas

1. **involve** : concern, include.

- Christmas Party and Dance
- Spring Dance
- School Picnic – all-day field trip
- Prom – an important dance before the summer vacation

Most American high school students have a part-time job during the school year and a full-time job during the summer. Parents encourage their children to work because it's part of growing up and becoming responsible and independent.
Most high schools have a job list to help students find work. Teenagers are proud of their jobs!

1 **Are these sentences true (T) or false (F)? Correct the false ones.**

		T	F
a.	Scholastic learning is the only objective of American high schools.	☐	☐
b.	If you're a sophomore, you're in the second year.	☐	☐
c.	On Saturday, school ends at noon.	☐	☐
d.	Only athletes have lockers with combination locks.	☐	☐
e.	Students don't go home for lunch.	☐	☐
f.	After school there are clubs and activities for the best students.	☐	☐
g.	Cheerleaders wear special uniforms and coordinate the cheering at sports activities.	☐	☐
h.	High schools help students find part-time and full-time jobs.	☐	☐

For discussion and writing

2 **a.** Compare your school with an American high school. What are the similarities and differences?

b. Which aspect of the American high school do you like best? Which do you like least?

c. Name three things you would like to change in your school, and HOW you would change them.

CHAPTER 5

Mr Stone

When the school day finished, Paul and I hid behind some bushes [1] and watched the school gate. We saw many classes go home, and some teachers. But we didn't see Mr Stone. The minutes passed. "Maybe he went home by car," I said.

At that moment, through the bushes, we saw a man with black hair and very high cheekbones walk past.

"It's him!" I whispered.

"Wait! He mustn't suspect that we are following him," Paul said.

We waited two minutes. "OK. We can go," I said.

1. **bushes** : 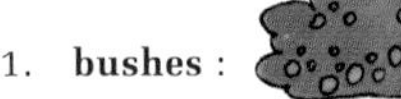

Mr Stone

We followed him at a distance and finally we saw him go into a house. It was a pretty, pink, two-storey building. There was a lawn [1] in front of it and a big tree on the side.

We crept [2] up to the window and carefully looked inside. Mr Stone put his briefcase down and opened the refrigerator. He took out another bottle of that horrible green liquid and put it on the table. Then he went upstairs.

"Now what can we do?" Paul whispered.

"No problem! I can climb the tree!" I said.

"Are you sure?"

"Of course. Don't forget I play volleyball!"

"Be careful!"

I went to the tree. It wasn't very high and it was easy to climb. From my position I could see his room. Mr Stone was there.

"What's happening?" whispered Paul.

"He's sitting in front of a mirror," I said softly. "His hands are on his head... Oh no!!!"

"What? What?" asked Paul.

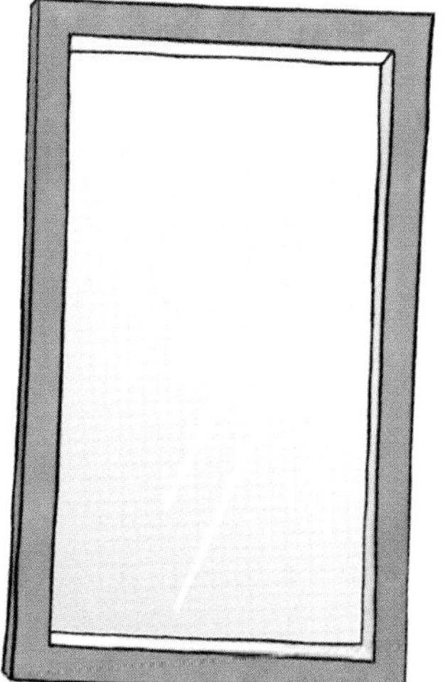

1. **lawn** : piece of flat ground covered with cut grass.
2. **crept** : (creep, crept, crept) moved slowly and quietly with the body close to the ground.

Alien at School

The teacher was totally bald,[1] and his head was covered with disgusting, brown warts![2] I felt sick.

Suddenly I noticed my reflection in Mr Stone's mirror and Mr Stone noticed it, too! He brusquely turned around and stared at me. I was paralysed with fear. My mouth fell open. I was expecting the worst. Instead, Mr Stone didn't look angry. He actually seemed very sad. He opened the window.

"You students think I'm weird. Come inside. I want to tell you something."

"Uh, Mr Stone, I'm terribly sorry... ," I started to say. I was extremely embarrassed.

"Don't worry. Since you're here, please come in."

I climbed down the tree. Paul was very nervous.

"Come on, Jenny, let's go away before it's too late!"

"No, Paul. I'm going in."

"But... ," I went towards Mr Stone's front door, so Paul followed. The teacher opened the door and made us sit down in his living room.

1. **bald** [bɔːld]: with little or no hair on the head.
2. **warts** : small, hard protuberances on the face or hands.

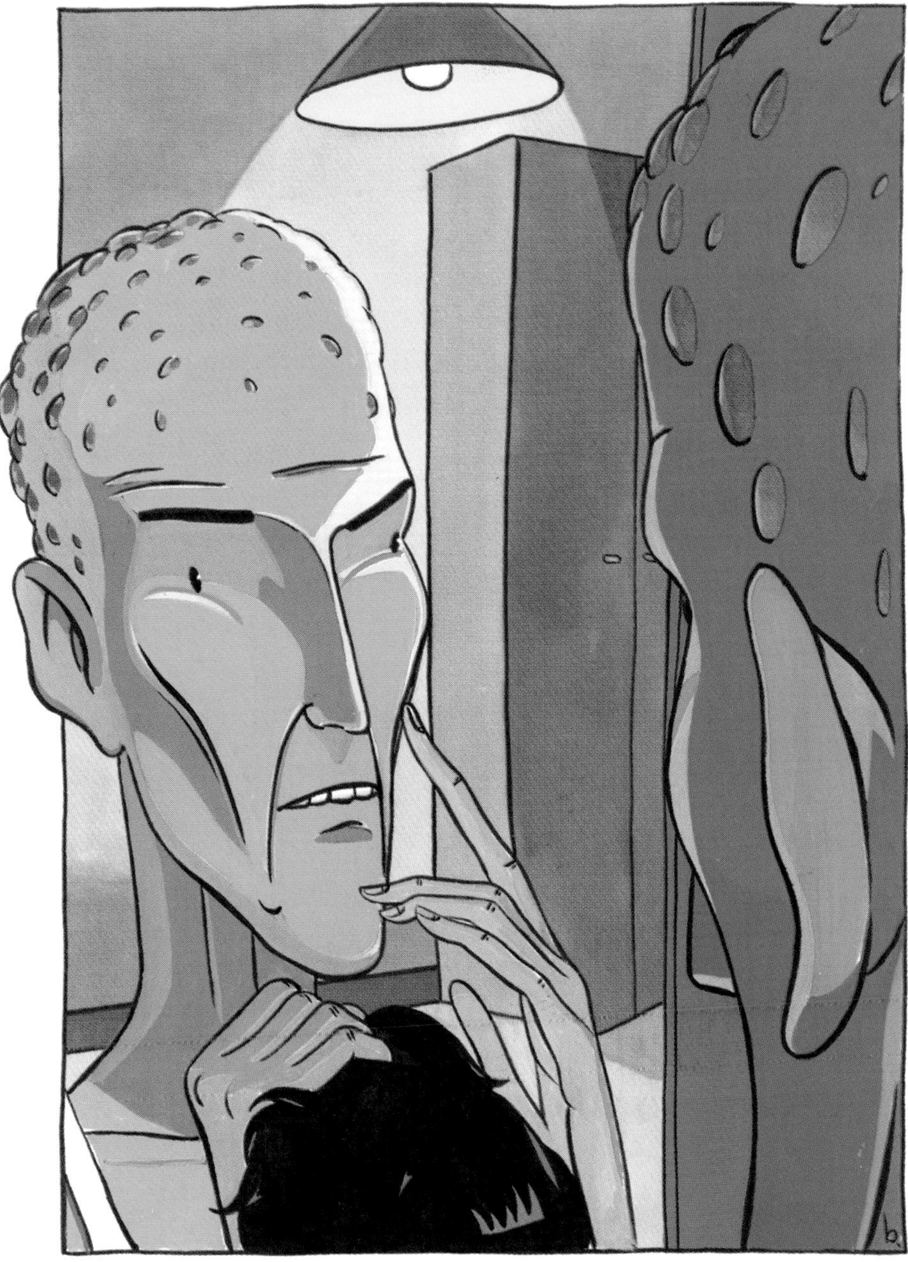

Alien at School

"Do you want something to drink?" he asked.

"No, nothing, thank you," I answered.

"W-What are those... warts on your head?" asked Paul, ignoring the look I gave him.

"These warts are the results of a throat [1] tumour. You see, I started smoking as a teenager and I continued until the tumour. Chemotherapy made me lose all of my hair, and I developed these warts.

"You've probably noticed my voice. Unfortunately, the tumour destroyed my vocal chords. So now I speak with a voice implant.

"The tumour has caused very serious changes in my life. I started to suffer from depression and I still see a psychiatrist. I also moved, hoping to start a better life in a

1. **throat** :  the back of the mouth.

new environment. In fact, I'm from Wisconsin. You see, I'm not married, and the illness has made me very lonely. People don't like illnesses; they stay away from sick people. Sick people bother them."

"Mr Stone, we really feel terrible about our behaviour," I said.

"Yes, we really apologise. We hope you can forgive us," added Paul.

"Don't worry! In a sense, I'm glad this happened. I haven't talked like this to anyone for a long time. You see, I want to be friends with my students. That's why I asked your class so many questions. But it's very hard for me to smile, or be cheerful. Try to understand, if I'm strict [1] or unpleasant."

I smiled at Mr Stone. I was very moved. [2]

"We understand," I said softly.

"May I ask you a question?" said Paul.

"Paul!" I exclaimed.

"It's OK. Ask me anything you want," answered Mr Stone.

"What's that stuff [3] you eat at lunch?"

"Oh... Did that scare you? The green liquid and the black pills are part of my treatment. They include protein and other nutritional substances."

1. **strict** : severe, rigid.
2. **moved** : (here) felt compassion and sympathy.
3. **stuff** : material of any sort.

"And why, excuse my curiosity, were your eyes amber-coloured yesterday?"

"Well, I tried some coloured contact lenses. I wanted to do something different. I thought that a new look could make me feel better, but it didn't work."

"Mr Stone," I began, "I saw you at the park, this morning..."

"Gee, I probably appeared very strange to you, with all those movements!" he said. "My doctor suggested early-morning exercise, in fresh, clean air. You really have watched me these last few days, I must say!"

Paul and I looked at each other. We felt rude[1] and very silly. We were ashamed for being so inconsiderate.

"Well, Mr Stone, we don't know how to thank you for your hospitality and kindness," I said. "We really don't deserve it. Our behaviour..."

"That's enough, that's enough, don't worry. Thank you for your company. I'll see you tomorrow at school. And remember, if you ever want to come and visit me, you're always welcome."

1. **rude** : impolite.

Mr Stone

"Thank you very much. We'll come again," said Paul.

Paul and I left Mr Stone's house, and walked home.

"Well, I think we've learned a lesson," Paul said. "We must remember that many people in this world are suffering; many people have problems; and, if they act in strange ways, there are reasons. There isn't an alien behind every bush. There's a person, just like you and me. And maybe this person needs friendship and a helping hand."

I looked at Paul with affection and admiration. His words expressed my own thoughts perfectly. We had let our imagination and superficiality dominate us. This made us forget human feelings and problems. I thought about Mr Adams and his artificial arm. Even in that case I had overreacted with my ridiculous suspicions.

"Hey, Paul," I said. "I want to celebrate! This adventure is over. I feel relieved. Let's go to the "Rainbow" and buy an ice-cream."

"OK, Jenny! Good idea!"

"Let's call Dana, too!" I added, thinking it was the moment to inform her about everything.

"Sure!"

We stopped at Dana's house and invited her.

What happened in Chapter Five?

1 **a.** Describe Mr Stone's head.
b. What happened when Jenny was in the tree?
c. What caused Mr Stone's throat tumour?
d. Why did he ask the students personal questions?
e. Why did he drink the green liquid with the black pills?
f. How did Jenny and Paul feel after their visit with Mr Stone?

2 **There is something wrong with these sentences. Correct the error/errors.**

a. Paul and I hidden in some bushes.
b. He mustn't suspect that we is following he.
c. Finally we seen him enter a house.
d. He taked out another glass of that horrible green liquid.
e. He's seating in front of a mirror.
f. I start smoking as a teenager and I continuing until the tumour.

Who is it?

3 **Read the clues and discover who the person is. Some names can be used more than once.**

Mr Stone	Mrs Ching	Mr Adams	Miss Smith	
Jenny	Dana	Paul	Fred	Apollo

WHO...

a. is the arts teacher?	....
b. has an electric prosthesis?	....
c. plays volleyball?	....
d. teaches math?	....
e. belongs to a dance club?	....
f. likes math and astronomy?	....
g. smoked as a teenager?	....
h. has a dog named Fred?	....
i. lives with his father?	....
j. had a tumour caused by smoking?	....
k. has a cat named Apollo?	....
l. exercises in the park in the early morning?	....

For discussion and writing

4 **How do you react to a person who is ill, handicapped or different from you?**

Before you read

1 Listen to pages 55 to 57 carefully. Then listen to them again and decide whether the following sentences are true (T) or false (F). Correct the false ones.

		T	F
a.	At the "Rainbow" the three friends ordered sandwiches.	☐	☐
b.	Jenny and Paul told Dana everything.	☐	☐
c.	Dana laughed a lot.	☐	☐
d.	Jenny left her watch at the "Rainbow".	☐	☐
e.	The watch was a gift from her grandfather.	☐	☐

....

....

....

....

....

CHAPTER 6

Thanks to a Missing Watch

We sat down at the "Rainbow" and ordered three sundaes.[1]

"Dana, we have news about Mr Stone!" I said.

"Yes, although it's a very long story," Paul added.

We told her everything: the news on the comet and the intergalactic meetings; our plan to spy on Mr Stone; finally, the teacher's sad story.

Dana's expression went from surprised, to worried, to ashamed, during our tale. "Our class must be much nicer to

1. **sundaes** : 

him!" she said. "But this comet... maybe aliens *will* come to Earth!"

"Dana, please, I don't even want to *hear* the word 'alien'!" I exclaimed.

"Let's keep our eyes open for people in need, not for aliens!" Paul added.

"OK, OK, sorry!" said Dana.

From the window of the ice-cream parlour, I noticed that it was already dark. I looked at the time... my watch wasn't on my wrist! [1]

"Oh no! My watch!" I exclaimed. Then I remembered. "I left it in the gym! I took it off at recess, to play volleyball. I must go and get it!"

"But, Jenny, I'm sure that the janitor [2] will find it and put it in a safe place," said Paul.

1. **wrist** :
2. **janitor** : person who cleans a school or other public place.

Thanks to a Missing Watch

"I don't trust him. [1] That watch is so important to me. It was a gift from my grandfather. He's dead now, and it's the only thing I have of him. I must go to school immediately!"

"But the school's closed now!" Dana commented.

"No, not today. Mrs Ching is at school all evening, because she's preparing some math tests. I know because I heard her talking to Miss Smith."

"OK. Well, I'll see you tomorrow then. I have to go home and start my homework," Paul said.

"Me too," Dana added.

We left the "Rainbow" and I went towards Jefferson High. The back door was open. I went in. Our gym is on the ground floor, but I didn't go there directly. Something stopped me. I felt a strange sensation. I didn't know what it was. Something wanted me to climb the stairs and go up to the classrooms.

I felt afraid. The school was dark and silent. I shivered. [2] "Where am I going? Why am I climbing these stairs?" I thought. My

1. **trust him** : (here) know if he's reliable.
2. **shivered** : shook or trembled from cold or fear.

heart beat faster and faster. Something terrible was at the top of the stairs – I sensed it – but what? I desperately wanted to run away and return home, but I couldn't. The mysterious force inside me made me go on.

On the third floor I heard a noise. Someone was moaning! [1] As I passed by the janitor's closet, [2] the sound became louder. Someone needed help! I opened the closet. It was Mrs Ching! The old teacher was on a chair with her hands and feet tied. She was gagged [3] and her eyes were open in terror.

"Mrs Ching!" I whispered. I took the cloth [4] from her mouth.

"Help!" she said. "Someone is doing something wrong, and he, or she, is here now! The person is in disguise!" [5]

1. **moaning** : making a low sound of pain or suffering.
2. **closet** : Am. E., a cupboard built in the wall.
3. **gagged** : 
4. **cloth** : a piece of material.
5. **disguise** : something worn to hide the real identity of a person.

Thanks to a Missing Watch

"OK, Mrs Ching, stay here. Whoever it is mustn't suspect anything." I put the cloth back in the teacher's mouth and left the closet.

I looked around the second floor. I was terrified. Everything was silent. The long, dark hall was very frightening.

Then I noticed something: a light was on in the computer room!

I crept to the door. Someone inside was working on a computer. I could hear fingers clicking on the keys. Slowly, very slowly, I opened the door. Just a crack. [1] It was Mr Adams! He was typing a kind of code on the screen. Was it a password? Then he took a small, plastic object from his pocket. It looked like a key. He inserted it in the diskette slot. The screen blacked out... [2] It flickered. [3] Then something appeared: it was the face of an alien!!!!

The alien had a green head and big, red eyes. It

1. **crack** : very narrow opening.
2. **blacked out...** : became black.
3. **It flickered** : shone with an unsteady light.

didn't have hair and it didn't have a nose. Its mouth and ears were very small.

Then Mr Adams put his hands on his head. He was pulling at his hair. It started to come apart! He was taking off his hair, and his face! A green, bald head surfaced: I realised that he was identical to the alien on the screen! He put his "face" on the computer table.

Then the false Mr Adams started talking.

"Klyreg calls base. Klyreg here. Klyreg calls base."

"ALTANK PILLEX, Klyreg. How is your mission proceeding?" said the alien on the screen with a mechanical voice.

"For now everything is OK. But I'm already tired of this mask, and I hate speaking this barbarian language!"

"English is not a barbarian language!" I thought angrily.

"I'm sorry, but your voice implant must stay inside you until the mission has finished. Then we can remove it. Tell me, does anyone suspect you?" said the alien.

"No, I don't think so. I had a small problem with an old math teacher, but I was in disguise, and I tied her up in a closet. So, everything's fine."

"Ha ha! You're wrong! I'm here now!" I thought.

"I hope you're right. Our mission can't fail. The spaceship must come this Friday. We'll land in the old, abandoned airfield. We'll wait for you there. By 9:30 p.m. you must be ready. You must have the two students to take to Mitrax. We can't be late. When the comet leaves the Virgo constellation, we won't be able to travel anymore. The intergalactic doors close on Friday, at midnight," said the alien on the screen.

"I know, I know. Don't worry. I must still choose the two students, but I think I know who I want."

"How will you capture the students? You can't touch them because you're electric."

"Aha! So the story of his prosthesis was a big, fat lie!" I thought.

"On Friday evening there is a family-teachers' meeting. During the meeting I'll leave the other teachers. While the parents are listening to the teachers, I'll ask the students to come with me. I'll invent an excuse. Then I'll take them to the science lab and I'll spray them with my

hypnotising spray. Once they're hypnotised, they'll do everything I say. They won't be able to think, or rebel. We'll go out of the building by the fire-escape exit [1] and walk to the airfield," said Mr Adams/Klyreg.

"I'm sure he wants me!" I said to myself.

"Be at the airfield by 9:30 p.m. then, Klyreg. Good luck. ALTANK PILLEX."

"ALTANK PILLEX, Gortz," said Mr Adams/Klyreg to the alien on the screen. Then he took the key out and the computer screen returned to normal. I silently closed the door and quickly went back to Mrs Ching.

"I can't tell you anything; it's for your own safety. Just act normally, and no one will hurt you," I said.

"Who..." Mrs Ching started to ask, but I escaped down the stairs and ran out of the building.

I stopped running when I was far from the school. My watch was still in the gym, but at that point I didn't care.

I had a lot of difficulty sleeping that night. I decided to tell Paul and Dana, but no one else: no one would believe me.

1. **fire-escape exit** : metal stairs that lead down outside a building to the ground, used when there is a fire.

What happened in Chapter Six?

1 **a.** Why did Jenny go back to school?
b. Why did Jenny go up the stairs?
c. Who was in the janitor's closet?
d. What was happening in the computer room?
e. Where and when will the spaceship land?
f. What was Klyreg's mission?

2 **Circle the adjectives that best describe an empty school.**

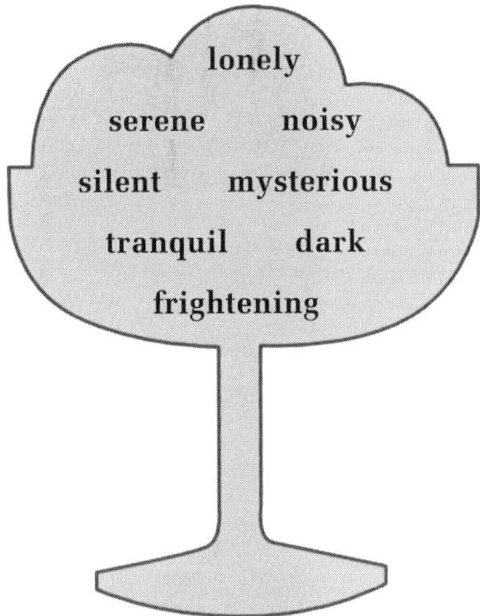

Now briefly describe how you would feel in a dark, empty school at night.

3 Have fun doing this crossword puzzle.

Across

1. person who takes care of a school
2. name of the math teacher
3. a kind of code
4. to put a piece of cloth around one's mouth
5. something that hides one's identity
6. the family-teachers' meeting in on ...

Down

7. name of the ice-cream parlour
8. a feeling
9. where aeroplanes land
10. artificial part of the body
11. Klyreg is an ...

4 **Look at these questions about Jenny and Mr Adams. Then write complete positive or negative sentences like the example.**

DID JENNY...

a. tell Dana the truth about Mr Stone?

Yes, she told Dana the truth.

b. forget her books in the gym?

....

c. go home when she left the Rainbow Ice Cream Parlour?

....

d. find a teacher in the janitor's closet?

....

DID MR ADAMS...

e. have a voice implant?

....

f. take off his face?

....

g. want to kidnap two teachers?

....

h. have an electric prosthesis?

....

Prediction

5 **Will Paul and Dana believe Jenny?**

6 **What do you think Klyreg will do with the students he wants to capture?**

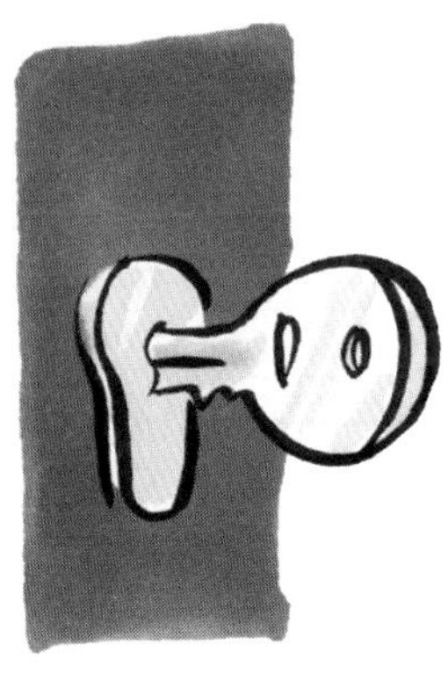

CHAPTER 7

The Plan

The next day, as soon as I arrived at school, I went to the gym to look for my watch. Fortunately, it was still there. At lunch time I took Dana and Paul to an empty table and started my story. I decided to get to the point immediately.

"Mr Adams is an alien!" I said.

"No, not again! Are you doing this on purpose? Because if you're not, you have a problem!" Paul exclaimed angrily. "I thought you wanted to stop all this. I thought you were ashamed of your behaviour! First Mr Stone, now Mr Adams!" he continued, while Dana raised her eyebrows incredulously and suppressed a smile.

Alien at School

"I know I seem crazy... ,"[1] I said, feeling tears in my eyes. "But I'm telling you the truth. I saw him with my own eyes! Please listen to me."

I told them everything, from my mysterious sensation to the conversation between Mr Adams/Klyreg and the alien on the computer screen. Both my friends looked terrified and shocked. They finally believed me. "Besides," I added, "do you remember how he looked at the sun? It's incredible!" I continued, "He's green and his name is Klyreg. Other aliens are coming in a spaceship on Friday evening. They're going to land in the old abandoned airfield near our high school. They want to take two students with them to Mitrax!"

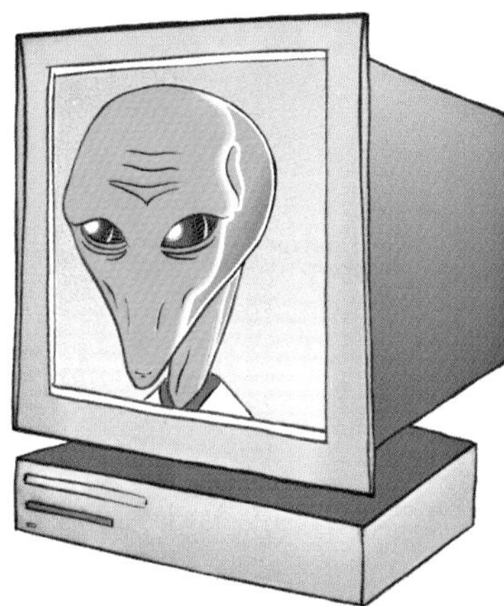

"Mitrax?" asked Paul.

"Yes. It must be the name of their planet."

"This Friday?" added Dana.

1. **crazy** : insane, mad.

The Plan

"Exactly. During the family-teachers' meeting. He's going to hypnotise them with a spray and take them on his spaceship."

"Today is Thursday! We only have a day to do something!" exclaimed Paul.

"I have an idea!" I said.

"What?" asked my friends.

"We can try to find the hypnotising spray and take it away from him. It can only be in two places: somewhere in his house, or somewhere in the science lab."

"Good idea! This afternoon after he goes home, we can look for the spray in the lab; if the spray isn't there, tomorrow morning we won't go to school. We'll get into his house in some way and take the spray," added Paul.

"But we don't even know where he lives!" objected Dana.

"Well, we'll find out!" I said.

"So we want to steal his hypnotising spray. Maybe Matt can help us. He has a key that opens all doors," Dana said. Dana's brother Matt is a policeman.

"Are you sure he'll give it to you? I don't think he'll believe this story," I said.

"Of course not! How can he believe something like this? I obviously have to steal the key."

Alien at School

"I hope he doesn't notice. Stealing a passepartout [1] from the police is a big crime," Paul commented.

"Yes, but it's the only way to enter where we want. Don't worry. I'll be careful. Gee, Mr Adams is so friendly and handsome! It's difficult to believe that he's a horrible, green alien! Well, this afternoon I'll get the key."

"Remember, don't say anything to anyone," I said. "This is our secret."

"OK. Don't worry."

"I hope everything will be OK," Paul said.

We went to our afternoon classes. I couldn't wait for the day to finish. I was nervous and excited.

1. **passepartout** : key that opens most doors.

What happened in Chapter Seven?

1 **a.** How did Dana and Paul react when Jenny said Mr Adams was an alien?

b. What was Jenny's plan?

c. Who was Matt and what was his job?

d. Why was Matt's key important?

e. What was Mitrax?

Odd one out!

2 **Circle the word that doesn't belong.**

a. computer keyboard spray screen diskette

b. aeroplane airfield jet pilot meeting

c. man parent mother father grandfather

d. science math arts test English

e. ice cream tennis volleyball football basketball

f. policeman mirror doctor janitor journalist

3 **Use the odd words to create your own sentences.**

....

....

4 **Using the given words, write sentences with** there is/there are, is there/are there, **and** too much **or** too many. **Look at the example. Remember, check to see if the noun is singular or plural.**

a. people/party

There are too many people at the party.

b. traffic/Boston

....

c. noise/classroom?

....

d. luggage/car?

....

e. children/library

....

f. news/television?

....

g. furniture/sitting room

....

h. sweets/cupboard?

....

Summary

5 Fill in the gaps in the summary using the words from the box.

difficult	**believe**	**alien**	**look for it**	**convinces**	**spray**	
science	**brother**	**need**	**key**	**steal**	**house**	**their**

At first Paul and Dana don't .... Jenny. But she soon .... them that Mr Adams is an .... They .... to find the hypnotising .... They decide to .... in his house and in the .... lab.

Dana's .... , Matt, is a policeman, and he has a passepartout .... Dana plans to .... his key so that they can get into Mr Adams's ....

It is .... for them to believe that .... teacher is an alien!

CHAPTER 8

Paul's Decision

I constantly thought of the day before. I remembered when he took off his face. Behind that blond hair there was a bald, green head. Behind those brown eyes, two red ones. And behind the nose, nothing! I shivered.

After school, I went with Dana to her house. Paul, instead, stayed at school to make sure that Klyreg went home. When Dana and I arrived at her house, there was no one there.

"I hope Matt didn't take the key with him!" said Dana. We went in. Dana went to her brother's room. I heard her open many drawers.[1] I crossed my fingers.

"Here it is!" Dana exclaimed.

"Oh, great! Now let's go back to school!" I said.

1. **drawers** [drɔːəz] : 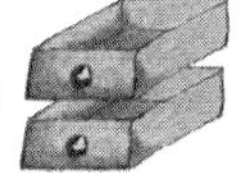

Alien at School

"Wait! My mom will be back soon. I have to leave her a note... I'll tell her I'm at the library," Dana said.

We went back to school. Paul was sitting on the steps.

"Has Klyreg left?" I asked.

"Yes. We can go in," Paul answered.

We went up to the science lab. When we arrived, we noticed that the door was open. Someone was whistling inside.

"Oh no! It's the janitor!" Paul whispered.

"Let's hide in the bathroom!" Dana suggested. "It's already been cleaned, so he won't come in."

We quickly entered the girls' bathroom and hid. After some time the janitor walked away. We heard him go down the stairs.

"OK, now!" Paul said.

We entered the lab and looked around. We opened the chemical cabinet with Matt's passepartout and examined every container. There weren't any sprays or strange bottles. So we tried the refrigerator.

"What's this?!" I said. Inside the refrigerator there was a spray without a label. It was very difficult to open and it had a bizarre phosphorescence.

"Wow! It's probably Klyreg's hypnotising spray! But how can we be sure?" Paul asked.

"We have to be sure that it's the right one. An error could be fatal. I have an idea! I can try the spray on my dog, Fred.

Paul's Decision

Fred hates taking baths and especially eating leftovers. [1] I'll spray him. If he doesn't protest, we have the right spray!" I said.

"Excellent! Please phone me after and tell me the results!" Paul said.

"I want to know, too!" Dana added.

We carefully went out of the lab and left the building.

When I arrived home, I prepared a big bath for Fred.

"Fred! Freddie!" I called. The dog was in the garden. When he saw me with the big basin full of water, he barked and howled. He ran inside his dog-house.

"Silly dog!" I thought. I took the spray, went to the dog-house and sprayed Fred. Then I called him again and I pointed towards the water in the basin. What a surprise! Fred calmly came out of the dog-house and

1. **leftovers** : food that remains after a meal.

jumped into the water! After Fred's bath I went to the refrigerator and took out some leftovers. I put them in his dish and gave it to him.

"Food time, Fred!" I said.

Fred saw the leftovers and didn't protest. He started eating. It was incredible! I immediately phoned Dana and gave her the good news. Then I phoned Paul.

"Hi, Paul. It's me. We have the right spray. Fred has been completely hypnotised."

"Great! Listen, can you come to my house now? I need to talk to you." There was something strange in his voice.

"Paul, are you OK?" I asked.

"Yes, I'm fine. I'll tell you everything when you arrive, OK? Please come. It's important."

I took the bus and arrived at Paul's house. He was alone, as always. He was in his room with his cat, Apollo, in his arms.

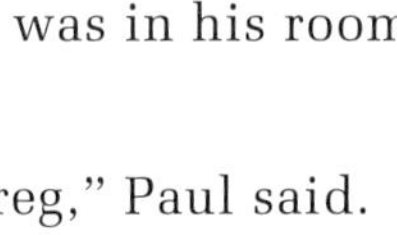

"I want to go to Mitrax with Klyreg," Paul said.

"What?!!"

Paul's Decision

"Yes, I want to go to Mitrax with Klyreg!" Paul repeated.

"Are you kidding? [1] You're crazy!"

"No, I'm not crazy. Look at my life. My mother doesn't love me. She went away and never wants to see me. How do you think I feel? My father is always working. He doesn't care if I'm here or in Timbuktu! He only cares about his young, blonde secretaries. At school everyone thinks I'm strange; you're my only true friend in class. Jenny, I'm not happy here. Try to understand. This world isn't for me. I don't like my life. I want to test my destiny and see what happens to me. Honestly, I really don't think that Klyreg wants to hurt us students."

"How do you know?" I asked angrily, shocked at what he was saying.

"He doesn't give me that impression. I'm sure the aliens just want to study us. I feel I can trust them. Also, you know I love space. I've always been interested in astronomy and alien life. This is a fantastic opportunity to see life on another planet, in another galaxy. This is my dream! This opportunity will never exist again. If aliens come to Earth at the next inter-galactic meeting, they certainly won't come to our town again!"

1. **kidding** : joking.

Alien at School

Listening to Paul, I started to understand his point of view. But it was terrible to think that Paul didn't have anyone. No one really cared about him. I was very sad.

"Running away to another planet isn't the right solution to your problems," I said.

"But I've tried to talk to my father about my problems. I've tried many times. Nothing has changed. Listen, I want to go to Mitrax. I feel it's the right thing for me. Something inside is pushing me to go."

Maybe going to Mitrax *was* the best thing for Paul, although I still couldn't believe it.

"If you're convinced... But I'll miss you, a lot. I'll never see you again," I said.

"Nothing is forever. You will see me again, I promise."

"Don't make promises you can't keep," I said, with tears in my eyes.

"Believe me, Jenny. Sooner or later, when the next intergalactic door opens, I'll return. And I'll have many new things to tell you!"

"Listen," he continued, "we must organise our plan for tomorrow evening! When Klyreg takes the two students to the science lab, he'll open the refrigerator but he won't find the spray.

"At that point he won't be able to do anything, because he can't touch us. If he touches us, he'll electrocute us," Paul explained.

Paul's Decision

"Then he won't be able to study us anymore!" I interrupted.

"Exactly. So, when he sees that his mission has failed, the only thing he can do is go to the airfield and leave with his spaceship. He can't stay any longer because he can't miss his spaceship. And the spaceship can't wait for him. I won't come to the family-teachers' meeting; I'll wait for Mr Adams at the airfield."

I sadly looked at Paul. "Good luck. I'll wait for you," I said.

Paul picked up Apollo and gave him to me. "I want you to keep him. Take care of him for me." He came closer to me. For the first time, we kissed. My heart pounded. [1]

"Oh, Paul, thanks for Apollo. Thank you very much." I stroked the black cat and he purred. [2]

1. **pounded** : (here) beat very strongly.
2. **purred** : made the sound of a happy cat.

What happened in Chapter Eight?

1 **a.** What did Jenny and Dana look for in Matt's room and why?
b. How was Jenny sure that the spray was the right one?
c. Who was Fred and what did he hate?
d. What was Paul's decision?
e. Why couldn't Klyreg touch people?

Synonyms

2 **Match the words in the box with their synonyms.**

wonderful	come back	chance	always	mad
particularly	weird	unhappy	complain	correct

a. constantly ....
b. return ....
c. strange ....
d. protest ....
e. especially ....
f. right ....
g. crazy ....
h. sad ....
i. fantastic ....
j. opportunity ....

3 **Complete these sentences with either the correct possessive adjectives or possessive pronouns.**

a. Paul's new computer had .... name on it. Everyone knew it was ....

b. "Where are you going, Dana?" "I'm going to .... dance club meeting and Jenny's going to .... volleyball practice."

c. "Who does this new science laboratory belong to?" "It's ....!" said the students, who were proud of .... new laboratory.

d. Matt put .... key in the drawer and said, "Please don't touch it. It's ....!"

e. "Is this watch ...., Jenny?" asked the teacher. "No, ... is bigger."

f. "..................... English test results were not good," said Mr Stone to .... students.

For discussion and writing

4 a. Give your opinion on Paul's decision.

b. Paul and Jenny are in love. But Paul decides to leave. Why do you think he does this?

c. Do you know anyone with a difficult family situation? Does he or she suffer from this?

d. Lack of parental attention and love can be a big problem for children and adolescents. On a scale of 1 to 10, where would you place this problem and why?

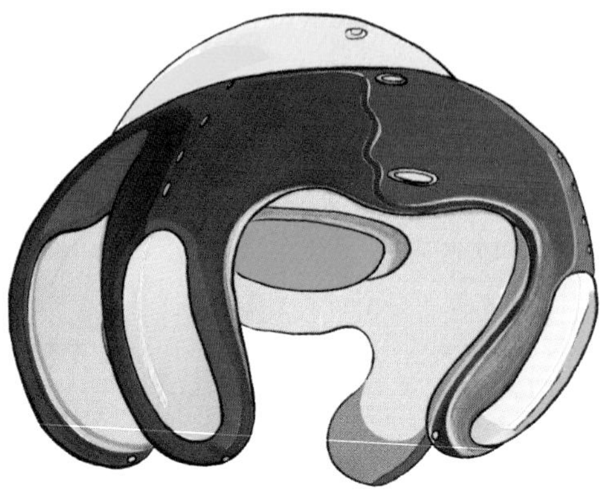

CHAPTER 9

Friday Night

I went back home and passed by Dana's house to give her the passepartout. That night I didn't sleep. I thought about the next day, about Paul's decision, about Klyreg. Apollo mewed in the darkness.

On Friday morning I got up early. I felt very tense. The day proceeded slowly. During the morning the principal came to remind us of the meeting.

"Don't forget that this evening there's the family-teachers' meeting. I hope to see all of you with your parents."

"Sure!" I thought. "And during the meeting one of your teachers will try to kidnap [1] two students and take them to a mysterious planet!"

1. **kidnap** : (here) take away a person by force.

Friday Night

When the school day finished, I went to the "Rainbow" for some ice-cream with Paul and Dana. Paul told Dana about his decision. She was obviously very surprised and disappointed. Those moments we passed together were very special. I will never forget that last afternoon with Paul. Our friendship seemed stronger than before. We felt more united because of our separation.

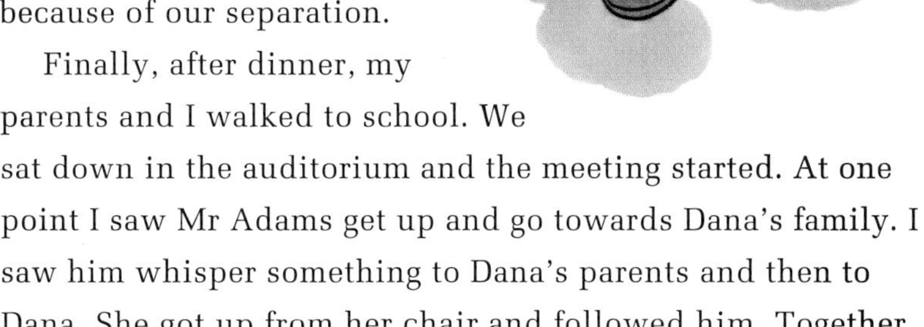

Finally, after dinner, my parents and I walked to school. We sat down in the auditorium and the meeting started. At one point I saw Mr Adams get up and go towards Dana's family. I saw him whisper something to Dana's parents and then to Dana. She got up from her chair and followed him. Together they walked towards Steven's family. Steve is another one of my classmates. I'm sure Klyreg chose him because Paul was absent. In fact I noticed him looking for Paul.

Steve, Dana and Mr Adams left the auditorium. "So he didn't choose me!" I thought. I looked at my watch: 9:05. Twenty-five more minutes. Suddenly I

had an irresistible impulse. I wanted to see what was happening. I got up.

"Jenny, where are you going?" my mom asked.

"I'm going to the science lab. Don't worry!" I said, and I quickly walked away. The door of the lab was closed. Inside I heard Mr Adams opening the fridge. I imagined his anger.

"Oh, no!" he exclaimed. "Where is it?"

"Where is what, Klyreg?" Dana asked. "Are you talking about the hypnotising spray? You lost, Klyreg!" she exclaimed triumphantly.

"W-What? You know...?" Klyreg was shocked.

"What spray? What are you saying?" said Steve, who didn't know anything about it.

"What courage Dana has!" I thought. Mr Adams had the power to electrocute her, if he wanted. It was stupid to make him angry. But in the end, it seems that Paul was right. Klyreg wasn't really a bad alien.

"Well, I don't think you need us anymore!" Dana said. The door opened and she walked out. "Come on, Steve. Everything's OK. Let's go back to the meeting!"

Then Klyreg came out. He seemed confused and helpless. I looked at my watch.

"Klyreg, it's 9:17. Go. Don't miss your spaceship," I said, almost with compassion.

Klyreg looked at me, even more surprised. Then he went to

Friday Night

the fire-escape exit and ran away. At that moment I thought of Paul. I followed Klyreg down the fire-escape stairs and out of the building. Our school is very close to the old airfield, so Klyreg and I reached it at 9:24. The spaceship was already there, waiting for Klyreg. Its portal was open, but all the lights were off. The aliens from Mitrax didn't want anyone to see them. Paul was there too. When he saw Klyreg, he ran towards him.

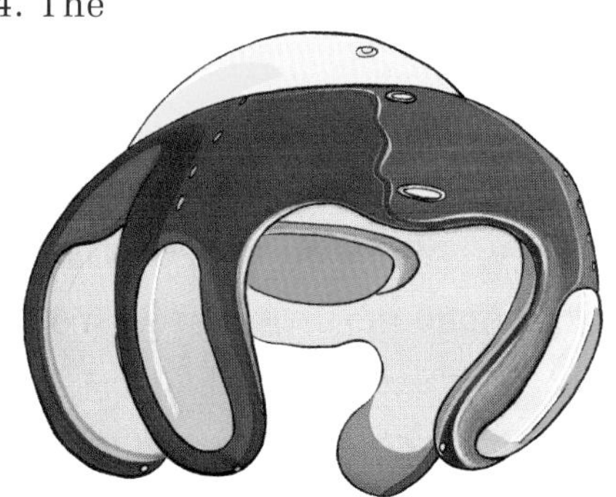

"Klyreg! Listen! I want to come with you! Take me with you! You can study me! I know you won't hurt me!"

Klyreg was literally shocked.

"Come then, Paul. Hurry!" he said, recovering from his amazement. [1]

"Paul!" I shouted.

"Jenny!" He ran to me and we embraced. "This crazy adventure has finally finished. Fortunately everything ended well for everyone," Paul said.

"Think about me sometimes," I said.

"I'll always think of you. And remember, I'll be back!"

1. **amazement** : great surprise.

"Paul!" Klyreg shouted. He was on the stairs of the spaceship. "The portal is closing!"

"Have fun in Mitrax, you space lover!" I said, laughing and crying at the same time. Paul went up the stairs and the portal closed behind him. The spaceship lights turned on and it silently went up into the dark night sky. I watched it disappear into the blackness. Then I hurried back [1] to school.

My parents were still at the meeting with everyone else. No one seemed to suspect anything. Dana and Steve sat calmly near their parents. I, too, went back to my mother and father, smiling innocently.

Today six months have passed. Everyone at school now knows the truth about Mr Adams, although not everyone totally believes my story. We have a new science teacher. Her name is Miss Lundberg, and for the moment she seems normal...

Dana and I have been to visit Mr Stone a few times, and his relationship with our class has really improved. He seems a happier person, and this pleases me a lot.

Steve is now Dana's boyfriend and they make a nice couple.

I still have the hypnotising spray. I keep it hidden,

1. **hurried back** : returned quickly.

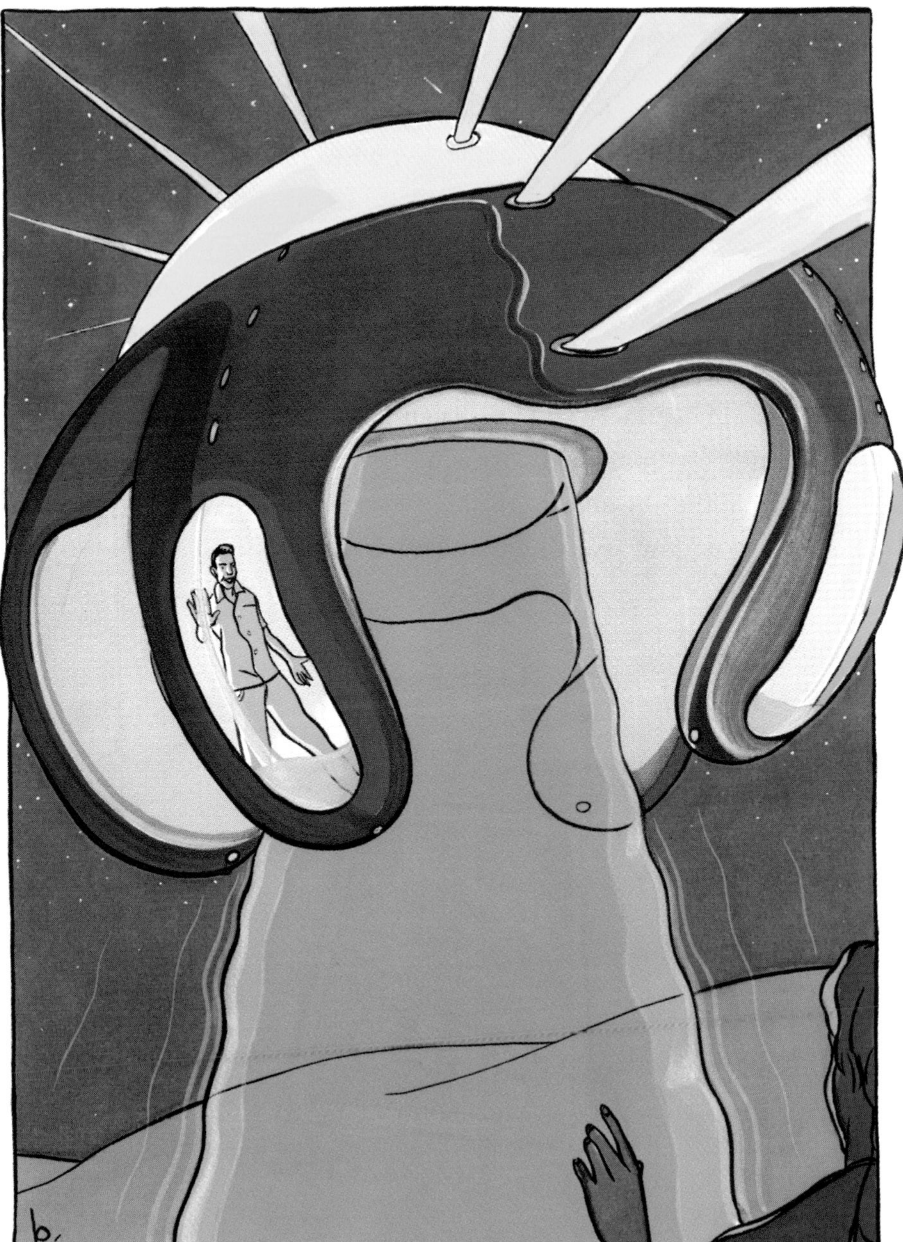
b.

although sometimes I use it on Fred when he needs a bath! Apollo is now a member of our family. Fred is a little jealous of him, but they're usually friends. I told my parents the entire story. They seem to believe me, especially because no one can find Paul. In the beginning his father looked for him, but he soon stopped worrying.

Sometimes Dana and I talk about Klyreg and our adventure. We remember Paul. On many evenings, alone in my garden, I look up at the sky and think about him.

"Good night, Paul, wherever you are. See you soon."

THE END

What happened in Chapter Nine?

1 a. Which students did Mr Adams choose?
b. Why was Klyreg shocked?
c. Why did Jenny follow Klyreg to the airfield?
d. What happened at the airfield?
e. Did Jenny's parents believe her? Why?

2 **Have fun with this crossword puzzle!**

ACROSS
1. relationship between two friends
2. encounter between parents and teachers
3. vehicle that travels in space
4. name of the new science teacher
5. Fred is .... of Apollo

DOWN
6. capture and take away against one's will
7. Klyreg's body is...
8. opposite of appear
9. a door, an opening
10. very surprised, amazed

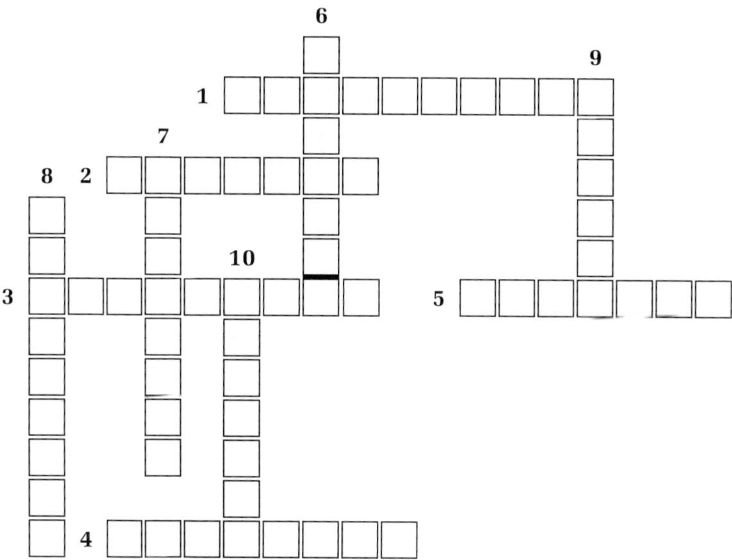

Summary

3 Fill in the gaps with the appropriate words from the story and you'll have a summary.

Jenny was a .... who lived in a .... near .... in the United States. During the .... days of ...., she and her ...., Dana and Paul, met their new ....

They thought Mr .... was very ...., because he had a .... and ate strange .... for lunch. Jenny, ... and .... thought he was an ....

They decided to .... him home and .... on him. However, they discovered that he wasn't an .... He was a man with a very serious problem: he had a throat .... caused by .... His voice was strange because he had a .... implant.

Everything seemed to return to normal. Then one afternoon Jenny forgot her .... at school. She returned to get it, and found Mrs ...., the .... teacher, tied to a chair in a ....

She discovered that the .... was Mr Adams, the .... teacher. His real name was .... He was planning to .... two high school .... and take them to ...., his planet!

By following a smart plan, Jenny, Dana and Paul were finally able to .... Klyreg. But Paul, who was .... with his life, decided to go to .... with ....

For discussion and writing

4 **a.** Calculate the month in which Jenny is telling the story.

b. What is your astrological sign? Check below.

c. Do you like reading your horoscope?

d. What are the characteristics of your sign?

e. Why do you think people value things or people more when they are about to lose them?

f. Have you learned anything from this story? If so, what is it?

ARIES
March 21 - April 20

TAURUS
April 21 - May 20

GEMINI
May 21 - June 20

CANCER
June 21 - July 22

LEO
July 23 - August 22

VIRGO
August 23 - September 22

LIBRA
September 23 - October 22

SCORPIO
October 23 - November 21

SAGITTARIUS
November 22 - Dicember 21

CAPRICORN
December 22 - January 20

AQUARIUS
January 21 - February 19

PISCES
February 20 - March 20

American Fast Food

When we think of American food we think of fast food. American fast food has become famous all over the world.

It's important to remember that Americans don't eat fast food *all the time*. Americans enjoy good, home-cooked meals. They also like going out to restaurants; perhaps a restaurant that serves foreign food, such as Italian, Mexican, French, Chinese, Japanese, Hawaiian or Indian! There are very many foreign restaurants in every town and city.

Fast food is perfect when you're in a hurry and you don't have much time to eat. Or when you're not really very hungry and you just want a snack. It is fast and inexpensive. Fast food is for everyone, from small children to grandparents!

Hamburgers and cheeseburgers are the most well-known fast foods. The typical American hamburger is made with good quality minced [1] beef, lettuce, sliced tomatoes, pickles, [2] onion rings, ketchup and a bread bun. [3]

1. **minced** : cut into very small pieces.
2. **pickles** : small cucumbers which are kept in vinegar.
3. **bread bun** :

If you add cheddar cheese, [1] then you have a cheeseburger. French fries and a soft drink [2] always accompany hamburgers.

Hot dogs are another typical fast food. A hot dog is a long sausage in a long bread bun. Hot dogs are often eaten at baseball games and other sports events. Fried chicken is another favourite fast food.

Did you know that America eats more ice cream than any other country in the world? The average American eats about 24 litres of ice cream a year! There is a great variety of flavours to choose from.

Americans love ice-cream sundaes (pronounced "sundays"). To make a chocolate sundae you need a big ice cream dish and 5 or 6 scoops [3] of your favourite ice-cream flavours. Then add a lot of whipped cream, nuts, chocolate sauce and put a red cherry on top! You can change the ingredients and invent your own sundae. Milk shakes are very popular too.

Do all Americans eat big breakfasts? Yes, most of them do. A big breakfast consists of fruit juice, fresh fruit, eggs, ham or bacon, toast with butter and jam, milk, coffee or tea. A lighter breakfast consists of fruit juice, fresh fruit, cereal, milk, coffee or tea.

1. **cheddar cheese** : yellow-orange hard chese.
2. **soft drink** : cold, non-alcoholic drink.
3. **scoops** : (here) balls of ice cream.

What do American families eat at dinner time, when they're at home? Dinner time is between 5:30 and 6 p.m. Dinner usually starts with a big salad. Then there's a main dish of either red meat, chicken, turkey or fish with two vegetables. Fruit and dessert follow the main dish. Typical American desserts are apple pie, pumpkin pie, lemon pie and cheesecake.

Americans drink a lot of milk. Children and most teenagers drink milk with all three meals. Adults usually drink at least half a litre of milk every day.

In all American cities and towns there are "cookie [1] shops" and "chocolate shops." "Cookie shops" sell all kinds of special cookies: chocolate chip, coconut, oatmeal, nut and many more. You can buy only one big cookie as a snack or you can buy an entire box of cookies! "Chocolate shops" specialise in different kinds of chocolate made in various shapes: chocolate pencils, chocolate books, chocolate animals and others.

Not everyone likes fast food, but everyone agrees that it's a lot of fun for young and old!

1. **cookie** : American term for biscuit.

1 For class discussion.

a. What are the advantages and disadvantages of fast food?

b. Do you like eating at fast food restaurants? Why / Why not?

c. Look at the foreign restaurants mentioned in the dossier. Which one would you like to try? Why?

2 Choose the correct answer.

a. Americans eat fast food
- [ ] at weekends
- [ ] all the time
- [ ] when they're in a hurry

b. Fast food is
- [ ] inexpensive
- [ ] unhealthy
- [ ] expensive

c. Hamburgers are accompanied by
- [ ] a big salad and a soft drink
- [ ] french fries and a soft drink
- [ ] a glass of milk

d. How many litres of ice cream does the average American eat during the year?
- [ ] 42 litres
- [ ] 24 litres
- [ ] 20 litres

e. In the United States dinner usually starts with
- ☐ a main dish and two vegetables
- ☐ fresh fruit
- ☐ a big salad

f. Typical American desserts are
- ☐ toast, butter and jam
- ☐ apple, pumpkin and lemon pie, and cheesecake
- ☐ chocolate milk shakes

A Personal Menu

3 What's your favourite:

a. fast food? ....

b. fast food restaurant? ....

c. soft drink? ....

d. ice cream flavour? ....

Compare your Personal Menu with your classmates, and determine the most popular:

e. fast food ....

f. fast food restaurant ....

g. soft drink ....

h. ice cream flavour ....